ISLAMIC ART

Frontispiece

BOWL

Painted in polychrome " minai "

PERSIAN, 13TH CENTURY

Diameter : 7″

Present owner unknown (ex Reiza Monif Collection, Paris)

ISLAMIC ART

One Hundred Plates in Colour

With an Introductory Essay

on Islamic Art by

RALPH PINDER-WILSON

NEW YORK · THE MACMILLAN COMPANY · 1957

First published in this Edition 1957

Text printed in Great Britain by
McLagan & Cumming Limited
Edinburgh

Plates printed in France by
Imprimerie Créte
Corbeil—Essonnes

INTRODUCTION

I

THE Islamic world, like medieval Christendom, was a society of widely different peoples sharing a common faith and a common attitude to life. Its art and literature no less than its social and political institutions have been deeply influenced by the religion of Islam. In the long procession of its history Islam has had to endure bitter internecine wars, political disruptions, religious schisms and enemies from within and without its borders. Yet in spite of so many vicissitudes its peoples have retained that outlook which distinguishes them from other civilisations.

Properly speaking, Islamic art is not a religious art as is the Christian art of the West. Quite early in its history the Christian Church took into its service the art of the pagan world in order to present visibly its doctrines. Pictorial representations of incidents from the Bible and lives of the saints as well as icons and symbols were intended to aid and strengthen the believer in the practice of his faith. With rare exceptions Islam has refused to avail itself of art for these purposes and to do so would be to oppose its essential nature. For to Muhammad was revealed the omnipotence and oneness of God and man's dependence on Him. If God chose to make His revelations through His Prophet, at the same time He makes Himself accessible to each of His creatures without human or material intervention. For this reason there is no religious iconography in Islamic art. Representations of the Prophet and incidents in his life and the lives of saints are rare ; and when they occur as in book illustration their purpose is neither to instruct nor to illumine. The appeal of Christian art is its humanity and constant endeavour to invest material forms with spiritual content. Islam on the contrary was hostile to figural representation and forced the artist to seek other ways of expressing himself. Orthodox opinion has taken the view that to create images of living creatures is to arrogate to human nature God's unique prerogative. That practice diverged from theory is evident from the illustrations in this book. Yet the official interdiction did not remain entirely a dead letter, for all images portrayed in Islamic art are but shadows of their living forms lacking solidity and individual attributes. The

7

three-dimensional representation of human forms is infrequent: and if animals are depicted in the round more frequently, the artist seems deliberately to avoid too lifelike a representation (16).

This partly explains why the ' easel ' picture—to be enjoyed in its own right —never enjoyed the vogue it had in the West. Portraiture and the ' genre ' scene appeared late and probably under European influence (99). Generally speaking the Muslim artist was not interested in painting from nature; he preferred to portray nature according to the forms long fixed in his imagination. In spite of a meticulous attention to detail, he succeeds only rarely in conveying dramatic or emotional tension, being content to evoke a mood by drawing on a limited stock of conventions. The exquisite painting of the lovers meeting in the moonlit garden breathes a spirit of magic and romance but the faces and gestures of the actors register little or no emotion (98).

Islamic art has been primarily concerned with the problem of surface decoration, with the result that pattern is often of greater consequence than subject. Discouraged by his religion from exploring the world of living forms, the artist transformed his visions into ornament of line and colour. So far from embarrassing him these restrictions provided a challenge which his imagination met by devising every kind of floral and geometric ornament. Even when he introduces human or animal forms, more often than not he subordinates them to the general decorative scheme so that they in their turn are reduced to decorative elements (5, 12). He proved himself astonishingly receptive to the arts of foreign cultures; from these he took elements which he then transformed and impressed with a distinctively Islamic character.

Typical of Islamic decoration is the arabesque, as its very name suggests. In origin it was a free interpretation of the classical acanthus scroll (54) and was developed in Egypt about the year 1000. In its earlier stages it retains a recognisable plant form but later becomes more and more divorced from nature. Yet however schematised, and provided that it conforms to the principle of the split leaf and continuous stem, it never loses its organic nature. Generations of artists devised beautiful variations on this single theme. The leaf may be round or triangular with its end pointed or tightly rolled; the stem may twine about itself, form spirals or undulate like a wave; but always the effect is one of rhythm and vitality.

Often the scrolling arabesque is used as a background ornament, since the Muslim artist invariably prefers to fill the entire surface with decoration. Besides the arabesque he incorporates flowers and trees and sometimes retains their natural and recognisable form such as the lotus (95), tulip (43, 67), dianthus (44, 73, 74, 77, 92), hyacinth (44) and cypress (79); at other times he

8

yields to his inclination for abstract pattern, producing strange and fantastic forms bearing little relation to any known flower (41, 42, 79, 90, 96) or combining them with animal masks (80). From the world of living creatures he depicted birds of every day occurrence (4, 9), the eagle (18, 61), and peacock (5, 62, 82), the ram (20), hare (35), horse (20, 27), elephant (14, 54), camel (8, 29, 54, 66) as well as beasts of prey including the lion (81, 83), leopard (79, 83), and tiger (79, 81), and wild animals such as the gazelle and ibex (62). At certain periods there was a vogue for fabulous creatures like the griffin (54, 55b, 56), the human-headed sphinx (frontispiece), the Chinese dragon and phœnix (69, 85) and kylin (83).

A recurring motive is the tree of life whose history can be traced back to the ancient civilisations of the Near East. In these earliest representations two guardians defend the tree from the attacks of wild beasts: the Muslim artist treats it purely as an ornamental device to which no symbolic meaning is attached even if occasionally the guardians or beasts are introduced (59, 61, 62, 64). It occurs on a vessel made probably by a Muslim potter in the Christian kingdom of Valencia (49) and even found its way into the repertory of European ornament. Other motives incorporated into Islamic art from earlier or foreign cultures are the guilloche (39, 45, 55a) and knots (39, 87), both common in Roman mosaics, and the Chinese cloud scroll (42, 82, 83).

Geometric and purely abstract forms had a particular appeal for the Muslim artist. Some, like the rosette (63a), may have developed out of natural forms. Favourite geometric figures were the pentagon and the polygonal star (34, 57a, 63, 89).

An original contribution of Islamic art was the decorative use of the Arabic script. Both the Arabic language and its script have a special significance in Islamic culture, for Arabic was the language in which God made His revelations to Muhammad. The task of transcribing the sacred text of the Quran has always been regarded as a meritorious one and calligraphy ranks high in the arts. Verses of the Quran were inscribed on the walls of mosques and on objects intended for religious and even for secular use. Other inscriptions are dedicatory (54) or contain laudatory or benedictory phrases addressed to the person for whom the building or object was made (13, 23, 49, 61, 62). The Arabic script with its rhythmic alternation of vertical and horizontal strokes is particularly well suited to decoration; whether the square and angular script known as Kufic (61, 62), or the round and cursive script known as Naskhi (23) and its graceful Persian derivative, Nastaliq (94).

When organising his decorative scheme the Muslim is careful to avoid giving undue weight or prominence to any single element. In the knotted silk belonging to the Victoria and Albert Museum (68) the sinuous floral scrolls are as important to the main design as the central scene. In the most successful compositions line and colour are combined with such mastery that, however complex the pattern, the effect is never restless or disquieting but always relaxed and tranquil to the eye. The principles of balance and symmetry are strictly observed; and vividly contrasting colours produce no sense of conflict (45). In order to achieve symmetry the artist uses reciprocal ornament in which one element mirrors another (4, 12, 23, 43, 58b, 91). When treated in this way birds and animals assume a heraldic character (frontispiece, 15, 54, 58a, 59, 61, 62, 64). On large surfaces such as carpets the design is divided into well defined areas by means of borders, polygonal panels, roundels formed of interlacings, and medallions (83, 85, 87-89, 92). A design is either complete and self-contained or a portion of an infinitely repeated pattern (87, 89). This idea of endless repetition made a strong appeal to the Muslim and the same motive underlies the friezes of running birds and animals (5, 20, 21).

The centres of civilisation were the political capitals and the great mercantile towns spread out on the important trade routes. In these cities the court of prince or viceroy and the merchant interest attracted artists and craftsmen by providing a market for the sumptuary arts. Organised industries were established where they were not already in existence. The greater part of the objects illustrated in this book was made for royal or rich patrons; for patronage, and above all royal patronage, was a decisive factor in the artistic development of the Islamic world and changes in taste and style often coincide with changes in dynasty.

Political frontiers did not prevent the constant interchange of artistic styles and techniques whether through the agency of traders and travellers—and the Pilgrimage to Mecca played no small part in the dissemination of ideas—or by political alliances or extensions of political power. The influence of metropolitan art reached provincial centres where it often combined with an established folk tradition.

Many of the details regarding the organisation of the arts in the Islamic world are obscure. There seems to have been no very clear distinction between artist and craftsman and the creators of much that is best in Islamic art remain anonymous. Here and there a name has been preserved (66). Potters put their names on bowls as early as the ninth century; and copyists often appended their names in the colophons of their manuscripts; but artists' signatures on miniatures are much rarer—the earliest known example is in a Persian manuscript of 1397. Not until the lapse of a century was a clearly defined artistic personality to appear—Persia's greatest painter, Bihzad, about whose life we know from written records and whose work has survived in a few precious manuscript miniatures. After Bihzad, artists' signatures are fairly common in manuscript miniatures and paintings from Turkey, Persia, and India; but with a few exceptions there is rarely enough material to make possible an assessment of any particular artist's style.

II

Within less than a century of the Prophet's death in A.D. 632 the Arabs found themselves the masters of an empire stretching from Spain to Sind. This empire was organised as a theocracy and ruled by the Caliph, Commander of the Faithful and successor of the Prophet. Until the middle of the eighth century the Caliph was drawn from the Umayyad family, aristocrats of Mecca, and ruled the empire from Syria. Arab governors administered the provinces in his name. The Arabs, whether townsfolk of Mecca and Medina or Beduin of the desert, possessed little or no material culture of their own : the conquered peoples, on the other hand, were the heirs of ancient cultural traditions. In Persia and Mesopotamia the Arabs succeeded to an empire that had rivalled Rome. The Sassanian kings of Persia had revived the glories of the Achæmenid empire of Cyrus and his successors; and Achæmenid Persia in its turn was deeply rooted in the ancient civilisations of Assyria and Babylon. Egypt, wrested from the Emperor of East Rome, had its long Pharaonic past; while the whole of the Near East had been overlaid by the civilisation of Greece and Rome.

For the provision of mosques, palaces and the sumptuary arts, the new rulers had recourse to artists and craftsmen from the subject peoples. For this reason the Umayyad monuments of Syria reveal several distinct styles. The Arabs utilised existing industrial establishments. In Egypt and Syria there was a well established textile industry and the Coptic weavers of Egypt now worked to the order of an Arab governor. The caliph, or the governor acting in his name, exercised the prerogative of rewarding a foreign prince or deserving official with a robe of honour or some rare stuff. The borders of these were often inscribed with the names and titles of the caliph and woven in a factory working exclusively for the court. The woven or embroidered decoration had of course to be adapted to the requirements of the new religion. The ' tiraz ' borders, as they were called, were attached to sleeve and neck-band with the pattern running horizontally. In the garment of the classical period the border had run vertically with a corresponding change in the direction of the design. Coptic and Syrian weavers often depicted people and animals; these had now to be excluded, at any rate on official garments.

A factory at Alexandria produced 'tiraz' bands embroidered with the caliph's names and titles; but other factories carried on the Coptic tradition of decorated bands. The roundel in the Musée de Cluny (58b) was woven either at Akhmin in upper Egypt where it was found, or at Alexandria or in Syria. Judging from its shape it must have formed the pendent of the 'clavus' band and was probably made for a Coptic tunic. It is one of a well defined group of silks, some of which are inscribed in Greek and others in Arabic. The design recalls the exuberant floral forms found in Persian stone and stucco carving of the Sassanian period. The pearl fillets surrounding the leaves suggest the jeweller's craft, and the same kind of treatment occurs in the mosaics that decorate the drum of the cupola in the Dome of the Rock at Jerusalem, also a work of this period.

In 750 the Umayyad caliphate was replaced by that of the Abbasids who established their capital at their new foundation of Baghdad and, as a result, political initiative passed from Syria to Persia and Mesopotamia. The subject populations, now mostly converted to Islam, vindicated their claim to participate in the government of the empire. The reigns of the Caliph Harun ar-Rashid, contemporary of Charlemagne, and his immediate successors were the golden age of Islamic civilisation and have been recreated for us in the pages of the Arabian Nights. From 836 to 883 the caliphs fixed their capital at Samarra on the Tigris; and excavations at this site have revealed a part of the splendour that surrounded the court. The pottery finds show that many of the techniques practised at a later date were already known at this period, notably that of painting on an opaque white tin glaze, in cobalt blue (2) and in metallic lustre.

Already the empire showed ominous signs of disruption. More than one governor threw off the yoke of the central government and succeeded in founding an independent if short-lived kingdom. Of the several Persian dynasties that rose to power in the ninth and tenth centuries, that of the Samanids in eastern Persia and Transoxiana was perhaps to have the most lasting influence. Their patronage of writers and poets contributed to a real renaissance of Persian civilisation. Something of Samanid art is known from the pottery recovered in the two chief cities of the kingdom, Samarqand and Nishapur. A bold and vigorous decoration is painted in coloured slip under a transparent lead glaze, a technique unknown in Mesopotamia. Kufic lettering and floral ornament are favourite motives, though birds and animals also occur. The same technique was practised elsewhere in Persia. The bowl in the Lewisohn Collection (1) was made at Sari south of the Caspian. Compared with the wares of Nishapur and Samarqand it has a decidedly provincial character which does not however detract from the charm and freshness of its design.

According to its inscription the beautiful silk tissue from the church of St. Josse (54) was woven for an officer of one of the Samanid rulers. This officer, Bukhtagin, was governor of Khurasan and the silk was probably woven in a city of that province, perhaps Nishapur or Merv. The St. Josse silk is the earliest dateable silk weave from Persia in the Islamic period : in style and technique it is related to a group of Sassanian silks and so provides evidence that the earlier tradition survived the Arab conquest.

Meanwhile, in the western provinces of the empire, political disintegration was even more complete. In 969 Egypt was conquered by the Fatimid Caliph who set himself up as a rival to the Caliph of Baghdad. The Fatimid dynasty based its claim to the caliphate on its descent from the Prophet's daughter, Fatima. The Fatimids laid out their capital a few miles to the north of the existing city of Fustat and named it Cairo, the Victorious. At their greatest expansion their domains comprised Egypt, North Africa, Sicily, Syria and the Arabian peninsula.

Contemporaries have recorded their impressions of the beauty and wealth of Cairo and described the marvellous treasures to be seen in the Caliph's palaces. Fatimid pottery, of which for the most part only fragments have survived, has rarely been surpassed. The lustre painted bowl in the Louvre (3) was made in a provincial centre rather than in Cairo. The arrangement of the portrait busts in roundels is in the classical tradition although the drawing is somewhat careless and summary. Fatimid art was especially receptive to Persian influence. The design of the birds sitting on the branches of an apple tree in another lustre painted bowl (4) occurs on a Persian silk weave of the twelfth or thirteenth century in the Rijksmuseum, Amsterdam ; and the little sprigs held in the birds' beaks are commonly seen in Sassanian silverwork. The plumage of the birds and the veining of the foliage is rendered by scratching away portions of the lustre, a style characteristic of a group of potters working in the eleventh century. Towards the end of the Fatimid period, the quality of pottery declined and the potter was often content to imitate the metallic tone of lustre by the use of glaze colour (5).

The silk tapestry bands of the Fatimid period are woven in a delicate range of colours and decorated with figural subjects, human as well as animal, and floral and geometric ornament. One of these (55b) is inscribed with the date A.D. 1056 in Kufic characters between a frieze of griffins and can therefore be dated to the reign of the Fatimid Caliph, Mustansir (1035-94). Towards the close of the Fatimid period interlaced ornament was popular ; the tapestry band

13

became broader and Kufic was replaced by Naskhi lettering, often debased (55a).

In Spain, which had been conquered by the Arabs and Berbers at the beginning of the eighth century, there appeared yet another rival caliphate when Abdur-Rahman III, a descendant of the Umayyad house, had himself proclaimed caliph in 929. The caliphate of Cordova inaugurated a brilliant phase of Muslim civilisation in Spain which was to endure until the last of the Nasrid kings was driven from the peninsula by the Catholic Monarchs in 1492.

In spite of its position on the western fringe of the Islamic world, Spain maintained contact with Persia, Mesopotamia and Egypt as well as trade relations with Sicily and Byzantium. Hispano-Mauresque art has a character all its own and reveals an astonishing power to absorb and assimilate foreign ideas : Persian, Mesopotamian, Syrian, Egyptian and North African. Byzantine and even Visigothic elements can be detected in Hispano-Mauresque decoration.

Silk weaving was introduced into Spain by the Muslims and silks were being exported as early as the ninth century. It is not always easy to determine which silks are of Spanish and which are of Sicilian origin, since Spanish silks were exported to Sicily where they were imitated by the Sicilian weavers. The famous peacock silk is generally accepted as Spanish although a Sicilian provenance cannot be entirely dismissed (62). The motive of the peacocks is certainly based on a Persian prototype though the style and treatment are quite distinctive and are similar to the presentation of the same theme in Andalusian ivory carvings of the tenth and eleventh centuries.

Sicily had early been occupied by the Arabs and later became a dependency of the Fatimid Caliph. In 1060 the island was captured by the Normans. Under its Norman kings, Palermo was the centre of a brilliant civilisation to which Greeks, Italians and Arabs contributed; for the Normans displayed a degree of tolerance rare at that period. In the famous Cappella Palatina built by Roger II at Palermo, Greek craftsmen executed the mosaic decoration while the beautiful ceiling paintings are the work of Muslim artists, probably Egyptians. Roger also founded a ' tiraz ' establishment where, at any rate in its early stages, Muslim weavers were employed. Many of the silks attributed to Sicilian looms are wholly Islamic in feeling (61). When the silk industry was introduced into Italy at the beginning of the thirteenth century, it was through the intermediary of Sicily that Hispano-Mauresque motives found their way into the early Italian silks.

In the twelfth century Andalusia was united to North Africa in the empire of the Almohads, Berbers of the High Atlas. Under this puritan dynasty figural representation almost entirely disappeared in favour of floral and geometric

14

ornament (63). One of the most interesting aspects of Spanish art in this period is the development of mudéjar art, that is, the art produced in the Christian kingdoms of the peninsula either by Muslim craftsmen or under Muslim influence. The mudéjar style was particularly strong in the ceramic industry. The great ceramic centre of Andalusia was Malaga which was famous for its pottery painted in lustre and blue. In the early fourteenth century Andalusian potters settled at Manises in the Christian kingdom of Valencia and instilled new life into the already existing ceramic industry. At first the Valencian potters copied the designs and techniques of the Malaga wares. To this period belongs the albarello in the Everit Macy Collection (49). The shape of this vessel was adopted by European apothecaries for drugs but was already known in twelfth-century Persia. The carefully painted Naskhi inscription round the neck of the vessel and the trees formed of large palmettes are common features in the Andalusian lustre wares. In the Louvre basin (51) the curling leaf is derived from the typical foliage of Almohad art.

By the middle of the fifteenth century the art of the Gothic north was beginning to make itself felt at Manises. The ivy leaf and acacia pattern of another albarello (53) are purely Gothic in feeling and reminiscent of the flower-strewn meadows of the Flemish and French tapestries. The dish painted with a leaping hound and inscription (52) is equally Gothic in inspiration.

Muslim power in Spain had dwindled to the Kingdom of Granada to whose enlightened rulers we owe the Alhambra, the latest monument of the Muslims in Spain. Yet even after the expulsion of the Moors, mudéjar art continued to be a source of inspiration. The silk in the Musée de Cluny (64) was probably woven after the reconquest of Granada but it retains Islamic elements in the lions flanking the tree of life and the simulated Arabic lettering. The spirit of the design however belongs rather to the Renaissance.

In Persia the Samanids were succeeded by another Persian dynasty that of the Buwayhids, the last Persians to rule in Persia for the next five hundred years during which time the Persians had to submit to the rule of the foreigner. These intruders were Turks and Mongols periodically driven from their homelands in the inhospitable steppes of Central Asia. Already in the ninth century Turks formed the caliph's bodyguard and several attained high offices of state. One such was Bukhtagin, governor of Khurasan, for whom the St. Josse silk was made. Up to this time the Turks came singly to offer their services to Muslim princes; now they began to appear in organised bodies intent on acquiring lands and power. The first of these movements was led by Mahmud of Ghazna who dispossessed the Samanids and founded a kingdom comprising Trans-oxiana, Afghanistan and north-western India. Of greater consequence in the history of Persia was the rise of the house of Seljuk whose leader Sabukhtagin secured control of the greater part of Persia and, by entering Baghdad in 1055, gained the ascendancy over the caliph himself. The Seljuk rulers whose empire lasted just over a century were zealous and orthodox Muslims. Under their patronage a particular style of art and architecture developed, and this continued under their successors, the Atabegs in Persia and Mesopotamia and the Seljuks of Rum in Asia Minor.

The twelfth and thirteenth centuries are the golden age of Persian pottery. Many of the refinements and technical improvements introduced in this period had already been anticipated by the Fatimid potters of Egypt. Seljuk decoration is alive with a nervous energy. Birds and animals move against a background of scrolling arabesques in which the split leaf is prominent. Even Arabic lettering acquires a sense of movement.

Stimulated by the fine Sung porcelains imported from China, the Persian potters discovered a way of producing a body clay harder and thinner than that of previous wares. One type has carved decoration like the Ting ware of China but is Islamic both in shape and in the style of decoration (6). Some vessels of this type are stained with a transparent glaze as also are the moulded figures of birds and animals (16). There were several ways of painting in more than one colour. One was to build a raised line between two adjacent areas in order to prevent the glazes running in the kiln (12); another was to apply a thin slip of black clay to the surface, removing with the knife those portions of the design to be left vacant and then covering the whole with a transparent turquoise glaze (14). Neither method allowed much freedom of drawing which was made possible only by the discovery of true underglaze painting. This technique, already known in Egypt (5), was practised by the Persian potters towards the end of the twelfth century. The ewer with its spout in the form of a cock's head (15) has an outer shell to the body decorated in open work. The features of the sphinx and details of the scrolls are rendered in finely drawn black lines; the handle and spout of the vessel and the band below the open work are painted in cobalt, while the entire surface is stained turquoise.

The art of lustre painting may have been introduced into Persia by migrant potters from Egypt in the second half of the twelfth century. The finest lustre wares were produced at Rayy, an important city in ancient and medieval times and near the modern town of Teheran, and at Kashan, 125 miles south of Teheran (19). In recent years a 'cache' of Seljuk pottery was found at Gurgan on the Caspian. The vessels were in the original packing in which they had been despatched from the factory. As a result they have retained their pristine freshness (21). The style of painting does not always quite accord with that of

16

either Rayy or Kashan and some at least must have been produced at a provincial factory.

The lustre technique gave the artist an opportunity of handling the surface in a surprisingly detailed and elaborate manner. Sometimes he even attempted narrative scenes. The same kind of treatment was possible in the so-called 'minai' or enamel technique. This was a purely Persian invention. In this process certain colours were fixed in a first firing while others unable to withstand great heat were fired at a lower temperature. 'Minai' wares were probably produced at Kashan, Rayy and Sava. As in the lustre wares, the painter often favoured the narrative scene. The goblet in the Freer Gallery (27) is enriched with scenes illustrating an incident from Firdausi's *Shah-Nameh* the national epic of Persia. The story is presented in three registers and tells how the paladin Bizhan went to seek out Manizha daughter of Afrasiyab king of Turan and won her love. Complete narratives such as this are rare and the more usual type of decoration consists of feasting scenes (25, 26), seated figures (32), horsemen (30), and animals (29). This type of decoration is very effective when placed on a turquoise ground (frontispiece, 31, 32). In some vessels the 'minai' colours are enhanced with gilding (25, 31) or with gilding and relief ornament (28, 30, 36). On a few rare pieces 'minai' and lustre are combined (22).

More provincial in style is a group of pottery found at Aghkand in northwest Persia. Vessels of this type are executed in the so-called sgraffiato technique in which the design is cut or engraved through a white slip to reveal the red earthenware body underneath; glaze colours were then added (10, 11). Another type is the so-called Garrus ware, examples of which were found in the district of that name south-west of the Caspian. In this the design was left standing in relief against the cut away background, the whole being covered by a colourless glaze with green additions (8) or a green glaze (9).

An extension of the Seljuk style was developed in Syria and Mesopotamia under the Seljuk Atabegs. The Syrian town of Rakka on the upper Euphrates was an important centre of glass and pottery production. Many of the Persian techniques were employed here. The drawing of the Syrian wares is broader and looser than that of the Persian wares. Besides the Seljuk type of seated youths and maidens, foliate scrolls and Arabic lettering, both Kufic and Naskhi, were favourite motives. The tone of the lustre which is sometimes combined with blue is a rich brown (23). Underglaze painting was also known (17).

Over this sunlit world there loomed the shadow of impending disaster. With a suddenness quite unforeseen the Mongol hordes emerged from their home in the high plateau of Central Asia and broke through the barriers of the civilised world. One after another the cities of Transoxiana and Persia went down before the conquerors who left a wilderness in their wake. In 1258 they entered and sacked Baghdad and slew the aged caliph. Persia and Mesopotamia were incorporated within the Mongol empire. This empire united the greater part of Asia under one rule, for in China the Sung dynasty was replaced by a Mongol dynasty. Unlike the Turkish invaders, who were already Islamicised before they started on their conquests, the Mongols were barbarians intent only on destruction.

With their cities laid waste and their irrigation systems destroyed the Muslims might well have given way to despair. As often in the past, so once again they were to prove their power of resilience. Like the Romans the Mongols succumbed to the blandishments of the conquered. The Mongol dynasty of the Ilkhanids was established in Persia and Mesopotamia and at the close of the thirteenth century the Ilkhanid sovereign was converted to Islam.

The Ilkhanids set out to rebuild the civilisation with the same energy they had devoted to destroying it. The unification of Asia made possible an unprecedented exchange of trade and ideas. The art associated with the Ilkhanids reveals a predilection for motives of Chinese origin like the lotus, dragon, phœnix and cloud scroll. Ilkhanid art however was considerably more than a taste for 'chinoiserie'; for the influence of China brought a more acute observation of nature which introduced into painting a greater naturalism.

Our knowledge of painting in Persia before the Ilkhanids is confined to a few fragmentary wall paintings and the decorative arts. Illustrated manuscripts certainly existed but, save perhaps for a single manuscript, none has survived. It was in fact under Ilkhanid patronage that the style of miniature painting associated with Persia emerged. Rashid ud-Din, Persian prime minister to successive rulers of the Ilkhanid house, established a scriptorium at Tabriz. He wrote his great Compendium of History for his master, Ghazan Khan; two portions of this work written during the author's lifetime are preserved in the Library of the Royal Asiatic Society and the University Library, Edinburgh. The miniatures are handled in a linear style with delicate tints, clearly inspired by Chinese painting and a style quite unlike that current in Mesopotamia as it appears in manuscript miniatures or that of the Persian 'minai' or lustre wares.

About the middle of the fourteenth century a manuscript of the *Shah-Nameh* was produced of which only the miniatures have survived, dispersed throughout the museums and collections of Europe and America. Some of these illustrations are among the masterpieces of Persian painting. The style is by no means uniform; in some it is the Chinese linear style that predominates; in others it is the colouristic treatment of the Persian tradition. This lack of an established style is well revealed in the painting of King Nushirwan rewarding the sage, Buzurjmihr (97). The stiff attitudes of the figures are in accordance with the tradition of Mesopotamian painting, while the rendering of the tree trunk that cuts across the foreground is purely Chinese. It is in the tragic scenes above all that the artist has risen to the height of the great epic. Out-stretched arms or a body bent by sorrow have caught the moment of grief and anguish. It is a curious fact that this same sense of the dramatic occurs in certain Chinese paintings of the Yuan period.

The great ceramic centres destroyed by the Mongols were soon replaced by others. By the end of the century Sultanabad, between Kashan and Hamadan, had become one of the main production centres, adopting many of the techniques of Rayy and Kashan. The large vase in the Hermitage Museum, Leningrad (20), has much in common with the Kashan wares, notably the way of reserving the moulded figures in lustre. The naturalistic trees and shrubs and the fine rendering of the buck suggest a late date in the thirteenth century when Mongol influence was already making itself felt in pottery decoration.

The 'minai' technique was replaced by one in which painting was restricted to overglaze enamels—white, red and leaf gold—applied to a surface of a brilliant blue derived from lapis lazuli ('lajvard' in Persian). Decoration consists of foliage or geometric ornament (33, 34). From Sultanabad, too, comes a group of wares painted in two shades of blue and black under the glaze on a white ground (35).

At the end of the fourteenth century Persia and Mesopotamia were the victims of yet another invasion, this time by Turcised tribes led by Timur, or Tamerlane as he is known in European tradition. His conquests however caused only a temporary setback to Persian civilisation which profited by the energy and resourcefulness displayed by his successors. Herat in Afghanistan and Samarqand became the chief cities of the Timurid empire. Herat, under the enlightened patronage of Baysunqur, grandson of Timur, became the resort of poets, scholars and artists. In Baysunqur's academy were produced some of the finest books of all times. The painting of the Meeting of Humay and Humayun (98) was made at Herat probably during Baysunqur's governorship and comes from a manuscript of the poems of the Persian poet, Khwaju of Kirman. Here we are face to face with a fully developed and assured style, so truly Persian that its essential features were to persist for close on two centuries. The artist has at last achieved a sense of harmony between man and the larger world of nature: the lovers and the attendants of the princess are no longer the sole objects of interest in a scene where all the beauties of a Persian landscape scene are depicted with loving care.

Politically Egypt and Syria were not greatly affected by the Mongol and Timurid invasions. The Fatimid caliphate was destroyed by Saladin in 1171; and he and his successors ruled these countries in the name of the Caliph of Baghdad until 1260 when the Ayyubids, as they were called, were replaced by the Mamluk or Slave dynasties. Ayyubid art developed out of Fatimid art, tending to emphasise the linear element in design; a process still further developed in the art of the Mamluk period. Figural subjects gave way to elaborate geometric patterns, stiff arabesque scrolls and the flowing Naskhi script. In ceramics lustre painting died out in Egypt but continued to be practised in Syria, where the fine albarello (24) in the collection of the Misses Godman was produced. The spiral ridges enhance a well conceived shape; the lettering, somewhat carelessly drawn, is used for its decorative effect and has no meaning. Typical of Mamluk pottery is a bowl in the Louvre, decorated in the sgraffiato technique with a dedicatory inscription probably to some Mamluk official and the blazon pertaining to his office (13).

The silk weave in the Musée de Cluny (59) belongs to the late Ayyubid period. Its design still shows Persian influence bequeathed by Fatimid art but the treatment is characteristically Ayyubid, paired birds between roundels formed of eight-petalled rosettes being common in inlaid metal work of this period.

In the sixteenth century the Islamic world was dominated by three powerful empires: the Ottoman empire, the Safavid kingdom of Persia and the Mughal empire of India. The Turkish House of Usman built their kingdom on the ruins of that of the Seljuks of Rum. By gaining a footing on the European mainland they were able to isolate the rapidly diminishing territories of the Byzantine empire; and when Mehmet II captured Constantinople in 1453 he found himself the lineal descendant of the Emperors of the East. Besides the Balkan peninsula almost the whole of the Muslim Near East fell to the Ottoman conqueror: North Africa less Morocco, Egypt and Syria, Mesopotamia and the Arabian peninsula. Unity of administration was accompanied by the spread of the metropolitan art and architecture of Constantinople to the provinces. By adapting many of the formal elements of the Byzantine church, the Turks created a wholly new style of architecture. Furthermore they were able to draw on all the resources of their empire for materials and crafstmen.

In the industrial arts the most important contribution was ceramics, textiles and carpets. The technical perfection of Turkish pottery and its brilliant polychrome decoration produce a splendid effect if these same high qualities sometimes induce a feeling of monotony—a danger inherent in all highly organised industries. The most productive factory was that of Isnik, the ancient Nicæa,

20

on the Asiatic shore of the Sea of Marmora. Its earliest wares were decorated in blue and white in imitation of the blue and white porcelain of China which had been exported in large quantities to the Near East since the beginning of the fifteenth century. Later, turquoise and green were added (39). Naturalistic flowers and vegetation first appear on vessels painted in blue, purple and a delicate sage green on a white ground (41, 42). Fantastic and exuberant floral forms are freely disposed over the surface.

About the middle of the fifteenth century Isnik began to produce pottery and tiles with a rich polychrome decoration which is given additional brilliance by a transparent lead glaze. The palette includes a striking sealing-wax red derived from a rare mineral substance found in Anatolia (43, 44). The naturalism of the flowers is offset by a strict regard for symmetry. This wonderful aptitude for flower drawing may have been the effect of similar floral decoration on the Italian silks and velvets that were reaching the Ottoman domains in this period, not to mention the influence of Persia where book illuminators were incorporating into their designs flowers painted in minute detail. Geometric and abstract patterns such as fish scales were also used by the Isnik potters (45).

After 1600 the quality of the Isnik wares declined though production continued into the seventeenth century. About the same time a factory at Kutahya in Anatolia began to compete with that of Isnik. Armenians were employed at Kutahya and many of the wares are decorated with Armenian subjects and inscriptions in Armenian. Some motives are clearly derived from the Isnik repertory; but by the eighteenth century designs were depending on folk traditions (46).

The silks and velvets of the Ottoman period are justly famous. Silk weaving was already a flourishing industry at Constantinople in the Byzantine period (58a). Factories had also been established in Asia Minor by the Seljuks of Rum. Turkish silks and velvets were being woven at Brusa in the second half of the fifteenth century and by the following century equalled if they did not excel the products of Europe. In some of the most sumptuous brocades the Isnik floral style was adopted; in others a more restricted colour range was used, the design consisting of a repeating pattern of large stylised plant groups (72). In the earlier velvets the design was often based on a broad ogival pattern but in the seventeenth century this was broken up into smaller units (73, 74).

Rug knotting is a very ancient tradition in western and central Asia; and was probably first practised by the nomadic tribes of Turkestan. It reached Asia Minor in the thirteenth century and the earliest surviving rugs of Anatolian origin are now preserved at Konya, capital of the Seljuks of Rum. In the

Ottoman period the industry was established at Constantinople and the towns of Asia Minor. At first the carpets combined the geometric tradition of the Seljuk rugs with the floral and geometric decoration of the Mamluk carpets of Damascus. Apart from the imperial establishments, manufactories were set up in the Anatolian towns. The most important was at Ushak which was already producing carpets at the beginning of the sixteenth century. Ushak rugs are among the most splendid of Turkish carpets (87-89). The arrangement of the design in medallions, the floral forms and the treatment of the border are inspired by the carpets of Persia. Designs are of the infinitely repeated type; in the so-called star type (87, 89) the position of each row is shifted in relation to that of its neighbour so that a diagonal pattern is obtained. In the medallion type (88) the position of each row is unchanged. Ushak rugs were highly esteemed in Europe where they arrived by sea at Venice, Genoa and Marseilles or by the land route through Transylvania. Europeans also placed orders in the Ushak factory for carpets in which their blazons were sometimes incorporated.

The highly stylised arabesque design of the carpet preserved in one of the Transylvanian churches (91) appears on carpets depicted in Venetian paintings as early as 1520 and in Dutch and Flemish paintings to the end of the seventeenth century. Carpets of this type contain features of the rugs of Ushak where therefore they may have been produced.

In the eighteenth century rug making flourished in the Anatolian towns of Giordes, Kula and Ladik. The most typical products of these centres were prayer rugs. In these the design is based on the prayer niche which in a mosque serves to indicate the direction of Mecca (92). It is remarkable that rugs retained their quality up to the last century, while the other arts began to decline by the eighteenth century with the accompanying political and economic distress of the Ottoman empire. The Smyrna carpet of the nineteenth century was a not unworthy descendant of the Turkish court carpets of the sixteenth century. One reason for this was that carpet making, apart from the imperial establishments and factories of the large cities, was a firmly entrenched industry in the villages of Anatolia.

With the collapse of the Timurid empire at the close of the fifteenth century, Persia's long period of foreign rule came to an end. Under the Safavid rulers (1502-1736), a dynasty of purely Persian extraction, Persia at last realised two centuries of uninterrupted prosperity. The sixteenth century witnessed the full flowering of the Persian genius, due in no small measure to the liberal patronage of this dynasty. Safavid civilisation was built on the foundations laid in the Timurid period; and Safavid painting developed out of the style evolved in Herat. The same artists worked for the new patrons in their capital at Tabriz.

Painting began to acquire a new importance, making its influence felt either directly or indirectly in the decorative arts. Towards the end of the century the manuscript was being supplanted by detached paintings often assembled in albums. In these, interest came more and more to be focussed on portraiture and the genre scene: and colouristic effect was often sacrificed to a rather mannered style of drawing.

Not very much is known about Persian pottery of the sixteenth century; but at the end of the century fine polychrome wares were being made in north-western Persia, perhaps at Tabriz. Most examples of this type have been found at the village of Kubacha in the mountainous district of Daghestan in the Caucasus (38). Some combine floral scrolls with portrait busts of youths and girls, rendered in the current fashion. Lustre painting was revived in the seventeenth century, after an interval of nearly three centuries, and in the best pieces the drawing is as masterly as that of the Seljuk wares (37).

The Persian genius can best be appreciated in the woven stuffs and carpets of this period. Silks with rich polychrome decoration were woven for use as court dresses, tents, hangings and cushions. Highly complicated weaves were used in order to give the desired effect. Some of the finest are woven with figural scenes after the design of fashionable artists: a lover leading his mistress captive amid plane-trees and blossoming flowers (65) or a youth idly drinking from a goblet, flask in hand (69). Another beautiful stuff in the Musée des Arts Décoratifs (66) illustrates the unhappy love story of Layla and Majnun: Majnun driven by despair into the wilderness where he is befriended by wild beasts while Layla rides by in her camel litter. This piece bears the signature of Ghiyath ud-Din, a famous weaver of Yezd, some of whose work has survived. About the middle of the seventeenth century an interest in flower painting developed and also influenced textile design. A gold brocaded velvet of this period (71) is decorated with a plant growing out of a rock, Chinese cloud scrolls and a butterfly in flight; its design must have been the work of a skilled draughtsman.

Persian carpets of the early Safavid period include some of the largest and most sumptuous ever made. The court encouraged an industry already firmly established in Persia. With a few possible exceptions (78) our knowledge of Persian carpets before the fifteenth century is derived from the types represented in miniature paintings. According to these, the early Timurid carpets were decorated with geometric patterns and borders of Kufic lettering. In the second half of the fifteenth century these were replaced by arabesques and floral scrolls arranged in medallions. This type of arrangement was evidently based on manuscript illumination and this association between book artist and carpet

23

weaver became even closer in the Safavid period when artists as well as illuminators supplied the weavers with cartoons to work from.

Carpets were produced at Tabriz where the manufactory was patronised by Shah Ismai'l and Shah Tahmasp, the first two rulers of the Safavid dynasty; and at Herat, Kirman and Kashan. From Tabriz comes a group in which the pattern consists of lobed medallions with hanging pendants together with animals and hunting scenes. A fine example is the portion of a carpet in the Musée des Arts Décoratifs (79), the other half being in the cathedral of Cracow. The minute rendering of detail and the rich variety of tones suggest a painting rather than a carpet. In the detail of a carpet in the Victoria and Albert Museum (83), the corners of the main field are occupied by winged genii. Although this carpet belongs to the end of the sixteenth century it is certainly connected with the great hunting carpets of the first half of the century. Some medallion carpets are decorated with inscribed borders and enriched with silver thread (82).

In a group of carpets of much smaller dimensions, the pile is of silk instead of wool; this imparts to the surface a shimmering effect (80). The main field is decorated with wild animals portrayed in vivid attitudes and is treated freely as in a painting. These silk carpets were probably made at Kashan. Among the products of Kirman in southern Persia is the so-called ' vase ' carpet in which the pattern includes one or more vases and a profusion of flowers and leaves rendered in bold colours (84).

A quite distinctive style was current among the nomad tribes of the Caucasus region between the Black Sea and the Caspian. Here an earlier tradition of animal design combined with the floral forms of Persian carpets. The angular and highly stylised drawing of flowers and animals and daring colour schemes all contribute to produce a splendid effect. In a carpet in the Victoria and Albert Museum polygonal compartments contain the death struggle of the dragon and the phœnix, so stylised as to be barely recognisable (85). In another, the pattern is composed of large palmettes with sharply serrated outlines (86).

The Mughal emperors, descended from Timur, united the greater part of India under one rule; and Hindu and Muslim combined in producing Mughal civilisation. In view of their origin it was only natural that the Mughal rulers were deeply impressed by the art of Persia. The style of painting current in Persia was introduced into India where it was modified by Hindu and later by European influence. This resulted in the emergence of a distinctive style. Periodically, however, contemporary Persian fashions were imitated (99).

The court also stimulated the development of the textile industry. In Mughal velvets the taste was for naturalistic flowers as in the contemporary Persian

24

velvets, but the difference in colour and drawing is recognisable (77). The same is true of Mughal rugs, the designs of which are often based on Persian proto-types but treated in a distinctive manner. An interesting fragment in the Musée des Arts Décoratifs (95) introduces animal-headed scrolls, a motive long known in Persia; the free and naturalistic rendering of the flowers and animal heads is wholly in accordance with Mughal tradition.

> *NOTE.* The fragmentary carpet on plate 78 was formerly in the George Hewitt Myers Collection, Washington. It is not in the Textile Museum, Washington, as stated, and its present whereabouts is unknown.

Persia dominated Muslim art but not Indian or Chinese.

25

THE PLATES

1

BOWL
Painted in slip under lead glaze
PERSIAN (SARI TYPE), 10TH – 11TH CENTURY
Diameter : 9″
Lewisohn Collection

2

BOWL

Painted in cobalt on tin glaze

MESOPOTAMIA, 9TH - 10TH CENTURY

Diameter: 7 7/8″

Musée du Louvre (R. Koechlin Bequest)

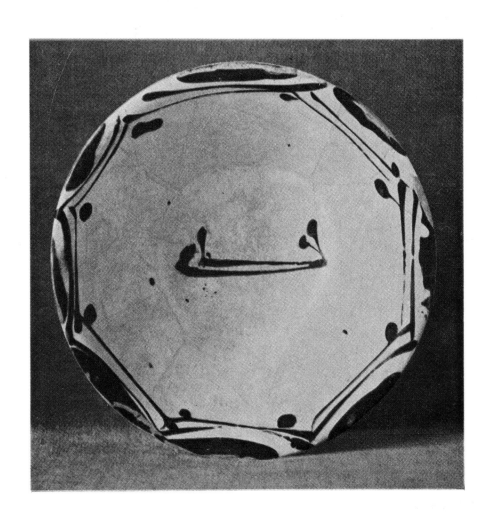

3

BOWL

Painted in lustre

SYRIAN OR MESOPOTAMIAN, 11TH - 12TH CENTURY

Diameter : 7 3/4″

Musée du Louvre (Mutiaux Gift)

4

BOWL

Painted in lustre

Found in Sicily

EGYPTIAN, MIDDLE 12TH CENTURY

Diameter : 10″

C. Côte Collection, Lyons

5

BOWL

Painted in purple under alkaline glaze

EGYPTIAN, LATE 12TH CENTURY

Diameter : 5 3/8″

Present owner unknown (ex Martin Collection, Stockholm)

6

EWER
Carved decoration with splashes of blue
PERSIAN, (KASHAN?) 12TH CENTURY
Height : 5 1/2"

Musée du Louvre (Mutiaux Gift)

7

BOWL

Carved decoration under turquoise glaze

PERSIAN (FOUND NEAR SAVA), 2ND HALF OF 12TH CENTURY

Diameter : 11 7/16″

Present owner unknown (ex Stoclet Collection, Brussels)

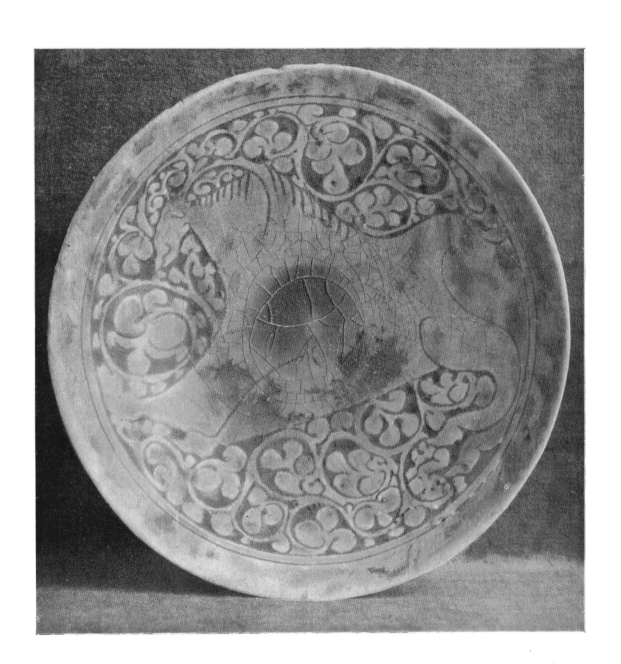

8

BOWL
Champlevé decoration under colourless glaze

PERSIAN (GARRUS DISTRICT), 12TH - 13TH CENTURY

Diameter : 9 7/8″

Present owner unknown (ex René Pottier Collection, Paris)

9

COVER

Champlevé decoration with green glaze
Found at Hamadan

PERSIAN (GARRUS DISTRICT), 12TH - 13TH CENTURY

Diameter : 6 3/16″

Present owner unknown (ex Martin Collection, Stockholm)

DISH

Incised and painted

PERSIAN (AGHKAND DISTRICT), 13TH CENTURY

Diameter : 10 1/16″

Present owner unknown (ex René Pottier Collection, Paris)

11

BOWL

Incised and painted

PERSIAN (AGHKAND DISTRICT), 13TH CENTURY

Diameter : 11″

Present owner unknown (ex Kelekian Collection)

12

DISH

Carved decoration with polychrome glazes ("lakabi")

PERSIAN, MIDDLE 12TH CENTURY

Diameter : 16 1/8″

Berlin State Museum

13

BOWL

Incised decoration

EGYPTIAN (MAMLUK PERIOD), 14TH CENTURY

Height : 7 1/16″

Musée du Louvre (ex R. Koechlin Collection, Paris)

14

BOWL

Black slip under turquoise glaze

PERSIAN, LATE 12TH - EARLY 13TH CENTURY

Diameter : 7 7/8″

Musée du Louvre

EWER

Pierced and moulded decoration with painting in black under turquoise glaze

PERSIAN (KASHAN ?), EARLY 13TH CENTURY

Height : 10 7/16″

Present owner unknown (ex Sambon Collection, Paris)

16

FALCON

Turquoise glaze

PERSIAN (SAVA ?), 13TH CENTURY

Height : 13″

Lewisohn Collection

17

VASE
Painted in black under turquoise glaze

MESOPOTAMIAN (RAKKA), FIRST HALF OF 13TH CENTURY

Height : 3 5/8"

Present owner unknown (ex Kalebdjian Collection, Paris)

18

DISH
Painted in lustre
PERSIAN (RAYY), LATE 12TH CENTURY
Diameter: 11 3/16"

Berlin State Museum

19

DISH

Painted in lustre

PERSIAN (KASHAN), DATED 607 A.H./1210 A.D.

Diameter : 13 3/4″

Freer Gallery of Art, Washington

20

JAR

Moulded in relief and painted in lustre

PERSIAN (KASHAN OF SULTANABAD DISTRICT), LATE 13TH CENTURY

Height : 2′ 6 3/4″

Hermitage Museum, Leningrad

21

EWER
Painted in lustre
Found at Gurgan
PERSIAN, LATE 12TH - EARLY 13TH CENTURY
Height : 7 1/2"
Musée des Arts Décoratifs

FRAGMENT OF STAR TILE

Painted in polychrome " minai " and lustre

Inscribed : The Iranians leaving the castle of Furud

PERSIAN (KASHAN), EARLY 13TH CENTURY

Height : 9 1/2"

Museum of Fine Arts, Boston

24

ALBARELLO
Lustre painted on blue glaze
SYRIAN OR EGYPTIAN, 14TH CENTURY
Height : 14 1/2″

The collection of the Misses Godman, Horsham

25

BOWL

Painted in polychrome " minai " with gilding

PERSIAN (KASHAN ?), LATE 12TH CENTURY

Diameter : 8 1/4"

Present owner unknown (ex Kelekian Collection)

26

BOWL

Painted in polychrome " minai " with gilding

PERSIAN (KASHAN), LATE 12TH - EARLY 13TH CENTURY

Diameter : 7 1/4″

Philip Lehmann Collection

27

BEAKER

Painted in polychrome "minai"
Scenes from the Shah Nameh (Book of Kings)

PERSIAN, LATE 12TH - EARLY 13TH CENTURY

Height : 4 3/4"   Diameter : 4 3/8"

Freer Gallery, Washington

28

FRAGMENT OF STAR TILE

Moulded in relief and painted in polychrome " minai " with gilding
Found at Rayy

PERSIAN, EARLY 13TH CENTURY

Height : 3 1/4″   Width : 4″

Present owner unknown (ex Martin Collection, Stockholm)

29

BOWL

Painted in polychrome "minai"

PERSIAN, EARLY 13TH CENTURY

Diameter : 7 7/8″

Present owner unknown (ex Engel-Gros Collection, Ripaille)

30

BASE OF BOWL

Painted in polychrome " minai " with gilding and moulded in relief

PERSIAN, EARLY 13TH CENTURY

Diameter : 4 1/2″

Present owner unknown (ex Kalebdjian Collection, Paris)

31

BOWL

Overglaze painted with gilding

PERSIAN, EARLY 13TH CENTURY

Diameter : 8 1/4 ″

McIlhenny Collection

32

BOWL
Painted in polychrome " minai " with gilding

PERSIAN, EARLY 13TH CENTURY

Height : 9 1/4″

McIlhenny Collection

33

BOWL

Overglaze painted with gilding ("lajvardina")

PERSIAN (SULTANABAD DISTRICT), 13TH - 14TH CENTURY

Diameter : 6 1/2″

Present owner unknown (ex Mutiaux Collection, Paris)

34

BOWL

Overglaze painted ("lajvardina")

PERSIAN (SULTANABAD DISTRICT), 13TH - 14TH CENTURY

Present owner unknown (ex Harding Collection, London)

35

BOWL

Painted in underglaze black, cobalt and turquoise

PERSIAN (SULTANABAD DISTRICT), EARLY 14TH CENTURY

Diameter : 7 11/16"

Present owner unknown (ex Mutiaux Collection, Paris)

36

EWER

Pierced and moulded decoration with gilding on turquoise glaze

PERSIAN, 14TH CENTURY

Height : 7 5/16″

Mrs C. J. Blair Collection, Chicago

37

BOTTLE

Painted in lustre and blue

PERSIAN, 17TH CENTURY

Height : 12 1/4″

The Collection of the Misses Godman, Horsham

38

DISH

Painted in polychrome

NORTH-WEST PERSIA ("KUBACHA" WARE), 16TH CENTURY

Diameter : 13 3/8″

Musée des Arts Décoratifs (ex T. B. Whitney Collection)

39

MOSQUE LAMP

Painted in blue and green

TURKISH, 16TH CENTURY

Height : 6 15/16″

Present owner unknown (ex Kalebdjian Collection, Paris)

40

TILE

Painted in polychrome

TURKISH, 16TH CENTURY

Height : 12 3/4″   Width : 6 1/4″

Musée des Arts Décoratifs

41

DISH

Painted in polychrome

SYRIAN OR TURKISH, 16TH CENTURY

Diameter : 14 1/8"

Present owner unknown (ex Stora Collection, Paris)

42

DISH
Painted in polychrome
SYRIAN OR TURKISH, 16TH CENTURY
Diameter : 14 1/8″

Benachi Museum, Athens

43

DISH

Painted in polychrome on white ground

TURKISH (ISNIK), 16TH CENTURY

Diameter : 13 7/8″

Musée du Louvre

44

DISH

Painted in polychrome on white ground

TURKISH (ISNIK), 16TH CENTURY

Diameter : 13 3/4"

Musée du Louvre

45

DISH
Painted in polychrome
TURKISH (ISNIK), 16TH CENTURY
Diameter : 11 5/8"

Musée du Louvre

46

VASE

Painted in polychrome

TURKISH (KUTAHYA), 18TH CENTURY

Height : 6 11/16″

Present owner unknown (ex Mutiaux Collection, Paris)

47

BOWL

Painted in green

HISPANO-MAURESQUE (PATERNA), 14TH CENTURY

Diameter : 6 11/16″

Musée du Louvre

48

VASE

Painted in green and purple

HISPANO-MAURESQUE (TERUEL, ARAGON), 15TH CENTURY

Height : 16 1/8″

Musée du Louvre

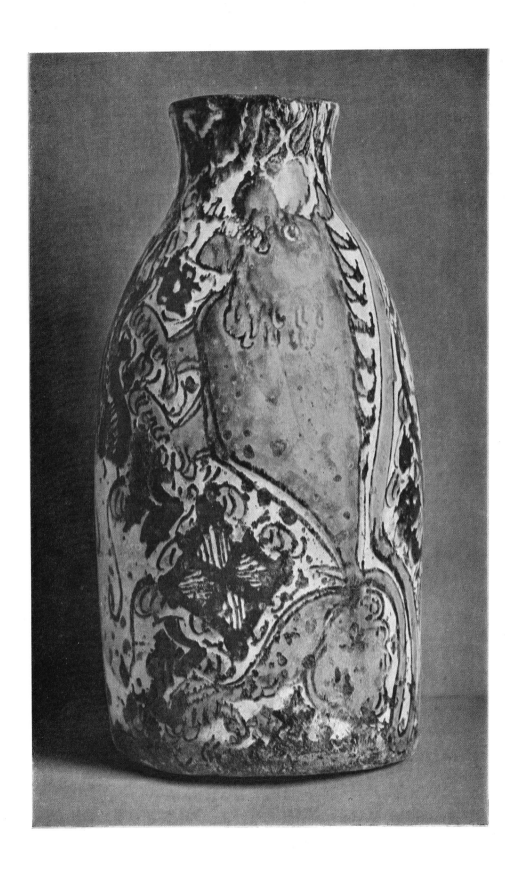

49

ALBARELLO

Painted in lustre and blue

HISPANO-MAURESQUE (MANISES), FIRST HALF OF 15TH CENTURY

Height : 11 13/16″

V. Everit Macy Collection, New York

50

COVERED BOWL

Painted in lustre and blue

HISPANO-MAURESQUE (MANISES), 1ST HALF OF 15TH CENTURY

Height : 10 1/4"

Instituto de Valencia de Don Juan, Madrid

5 I

HAND-BASIN

Painted in lustre and blue

HISPANO-MAURESQUE (MANISES), 1450-1475

Diameter : 18 1/2″

Musée du Louvre (S. de Rothschild Gift)

DISH

Painted in lustre and blue

HISPANO-MAURESQUE (MANISES), FIRST HALF OF 15TH CENTURY

Diameter : 14 1/2"

Instituto de Valencia de Don Juan, Madrid

53

ALBARELLO

Painted in lustre and blue

HISPANO-MAURESQUE (MANISES), SECOND HALF OF 15TH CENTURY

Height : 14 7/8″

Musée du Louvre

54

SILK TWILL

Inscribed : " Glory and prosperity to the Qa'id Abu-Mansur Bukhtagin, may God prolong his existence ". Bukhtagin was an officer of Abd-ul-Malik ibn Nuh, ruler of Khurasan and Transoxiana, and was put to death in 349 A. H./960 A. D.

EAST PERSIAN

Height : 20 1/4" Width : 3'

Musée du Louvre (Originally in the Church of St. Josse, Pas-de-Calais)

55

SILK TAPESTRY

EGYPTIAN (FATIMID OR AYYUBID PERIOD), 12TH CENTURY
Height : 4″   Width : 5 7/8″

Present owner unknown (ex Kelekian Collection)

SILK TAPESTRY

Dated 448 A. H./1056 A. D.

EGYPTIAN

Width : 4″

Musée de Cluny, Paris

56

SILK TAPESTRY

EGYPTIAN (FATIMID PERIOD), 10TH - 11TH CENTURY

Height : 4 3/4″   Width : 7 7/8″

Present owner unknown (ex Kelekian Collection)

LINEN TAPESTRY

EGYPTIAN, 11TH CENTURY

Height : 4″   Width : 7 7/8″

Present owner unknown (ex Kelekian Collection)

SILK TAPESTRY

EGYPTIAN, LATE 11TH CENTURY

Height : 3″   Width : 6 1/4″

Present owner unknown (ex Kelekian Collection)

SILK TWILL

SYRIAN OR BYZANTINE, 11TH CENTURY

Height : 5 1/2"   Width : 7 7/8"

Musée de Cluny, Paris

SILK TWILL

From the cemetery of Akhmin in Upper Egypt

SYRIAN, 7TH - 8TH CENTURY

Diameter : 6 5/8"

Musée de Cluny, Paris

59

SATIN

EGYPTIAN, SECOND HALF OF 12TH - 13TH CENTURY

Height : 9 7/8″   Width : 4 3/4″

Musée de Cluny, Paris

60

SILK TAPESTRY

MESOPOTAMIAN, 11TH CENTURY

Height: 7 7/8″   Width: 11 7/8″

Present owner unknown (ex Indjoudjian Collection, Paris)

61

SILK TWILL

SPANISH, LATE 12TH

Height : 9 7/8″   Width : 15 3/4″

Musée des Arts Décoratifs

62

SILK TWILL

SICILIAN OR SPANISH, 12TH CENTURY

Height : 9 3/4″   Width : 5 7/8″

Musée de Cluny, Paris

63

SILK AND GILT MEMBRANE TISSUE

SPANISH (ALMERIA ?), 13TH CENTURY

Present owner unknown (ex Kalebdjian Collection, Paris)

SILK AND GILT MEMBRANE TISSUE

SPANISH (ALMERIA ?), 13TH CENTURY

Present owner unknown (ex Kalebdjian Collection, Paris)

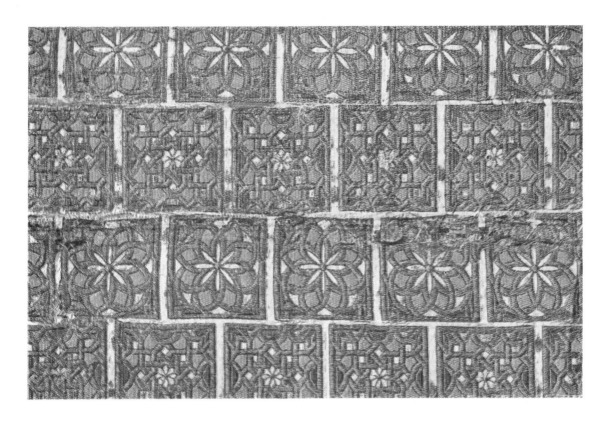

64

SATIN TISSUE

SPANISH, 15TH - 16TH CENTURY

Height : 7 7/8″   Width : 6 1/4″

Musée de Cluny, Paris

65

SATIN

Warrior leading a woman prisoner

<small>PERSIAN, PERIOD OF SHAH ABBAS (1587-1629)</small>

Height : 6′ 6 1/2″ Width : 23 1/2″

Musée des Arts Décoratifs

66

SATIN

Episode from the story of Layla and Majnun
Inscribed with the maker's name, Ghiyath

PERSIAN, SECOND HALF OF 16TH CENTURY

Height : 2′ 3 1/2″ Width : 11 3/4″

Musée des Arts Décoratifs

67

SILK TISSUE

PERSIAN, 16TH CENTURY

Height : 21 1/2"   Width : 7 3/4"

Musée des Arts Décoratifs

DALMATIC CUT FROM COPE

Scenes of Crucifixion and Annunciation

Knotted silk pile enriched with metal threads

PERSIAN, SECOND HALF OF 16TH CENTURY

Height : 4′ 11″ Width : 7′ 9″

Victoria and Albert Museum

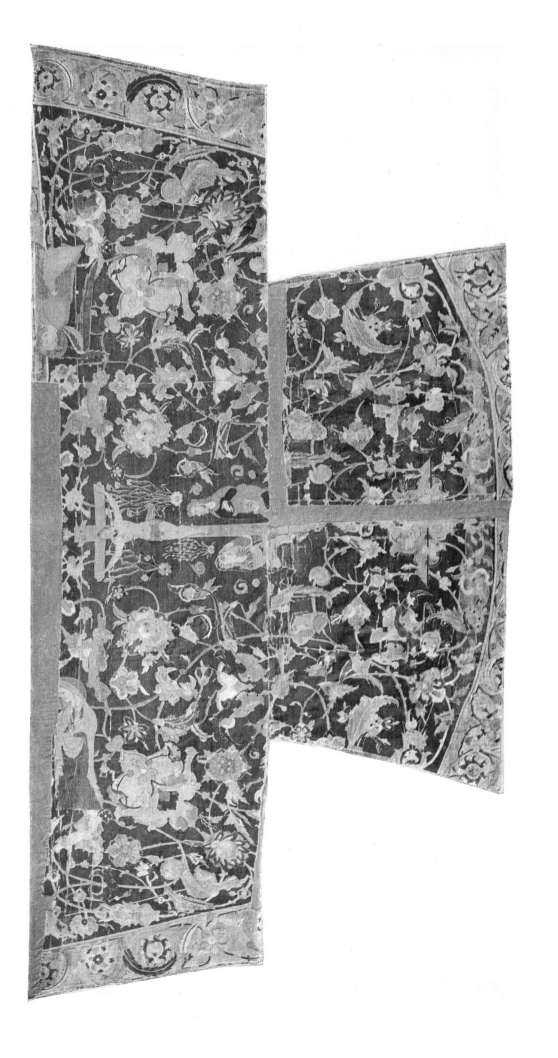

69

CHASUBLE
SIDE PANELS OF SATIN
PERSIAN, LATE 16TH - EARLY 17TH CENTURY

CENTRE PANEL OF BROCADED SILK
TURKISH, 16TH CENTURY
Height : 4′ 10 3/4″ Width : 2′ 3 1/2″
Musée des Arts Décoratifs

EMBROIDERED SILK

PERSIAN, EARLY 17TH CENTURY

Height : 23 1/2″   Width : 10 1/4″

Musée des Arts Décoratifs

SATIN VELVET, GOLD AND SILVER BROCADED

PERSIAN, FIRST HALF OF 17TH CENTURY

Width : 19 1/2"

Present owner unknown (ex Paul Mallon Collection)

SILK TISSUE

TURKISH, BRUSA, 16TH CENTURY

Width : 3′ 3 1/4″

Musée des Arts Décoratifs

73

SILVER BROCADED VELVET

TURKISH, BRUSA, LATE 16TH — 17TH CENTURY

Width : 3' 7"

Musée des Arts Décoratifs

74

SILVER BROCADED VELVET

TURKISH, BRUSA, 17TH CENTURY

Width : 23 1/2″

Musée des Arts Décoratifs

75

PRAYER CARPET

Silk tapestry enriched with metal threads

TURKISH, EARLY 17TH CENTURY

Width : 19 1/2"

Present owner unknown (ex Kelekian Collection)

76

SILK AND GOLD TISSUE

TURKISH, 17TH CENTURY

Height : 4' 6 1/2"   Width : 2'

Musée des Arts Décoratifs

77

BROCADED VELVET

INDIAN, 17TH CENTURY

Width : 2′ 7 1/4″

Musée des Arts Décoratifs

78

CARPET (FRAGMENT)

Silk pile

TURKISH OR PERSIAN, 15TH CENTURY

Height : 2′ 3 1/2″ Width : 13 3/4″

Textile Museum, Washington

MEDALLION AND ANIMAL CARPET (DETAIL OF FRAGMENT)

Wool pile

PERSIAN, TABRIZ, FIRST HALF OF 16TH CENTURY

Height (of whole fragment) : 11′ 5 1/4″   Width (of whole fragment) : 13′ 4″

Musée des Arts Decoratifs (Jules Maciet Gift)
The other half of this carpet is in the sacristy of the Cathedral of Cracow

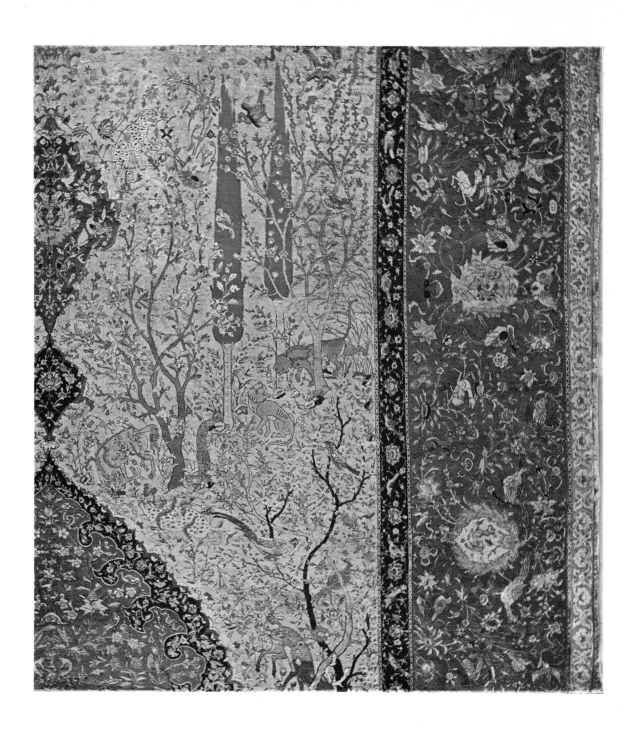

ANIMAL CARPET

Silk pile

PERSIAN, KASHAN (?), 16TH CENTURY

Height : 4′ 5/8″   Width : 3′ 6 3/4″

Musée du Louvre (Joanny Peytel Gift)

CARPET (FRAGMENT)

Wool pile

PERSIAN, 16TH CENTURY

Height : 15 3/4″   Width : 23 1/2″

Musée des Arts Décoratifs

CARPET (FRAGMENT OF BORDER)

Wool pile

PERSIAN, END OF 16TH CENTURY

Height : 15 3/4″   Width : 2′ 5 1/4″

Musée des Arts Décoratifs

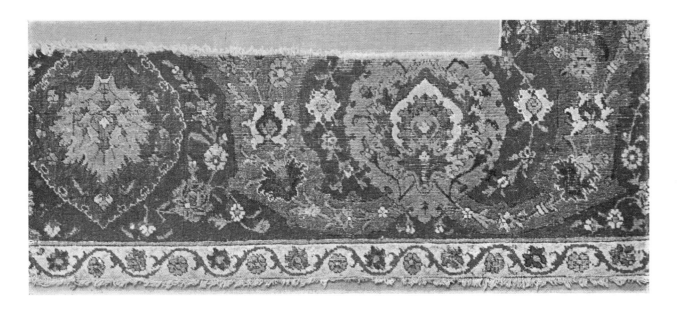

82

MEDALLION AND ARABESQUE CARPET (DETAIL)

Silk pile enriched with metal thread

PERSIAN, TABRIZ, 16TH CENTURY

Height : 8' 2"   Width : 5' 6 3/4"

Musée des Arts Décoratifs (ex Albert Goupil Collection)

83

MEDALLION CARPET (FRAGMENT)

Wool pile enriched with metal thread

PERSIAN, SECOND HALF OF 16TH CENTURY

Height : 4' 6"   Width : 3' 5"

Victoria and Albert Museum

84

VASE CARPET (FRAGMENT)

Wool pile

SOUTH PERSIAN, KIRMAN, EARLY 17TH CENTURY

Height : 13' 3/4" Width : 5' 6 3/4"

Musée des Arts Décoratifs

85

DRAGON CARPET
Wool pile
CAUCASUS, 16TH CENTURY
Height : 6′ 11″   Width : 6′
Victoria and Albert Museum

86

CARPET

Wool pile

CAUCASUS, EARLY 17TH CENTURY

Height : 5' 8 1/2" Width : 4' 1 1/2"

Protestant Church of Szepsiszentgyörgy (Transylvania)

87

CARPET

Wool pile

ANATOLIAN, USHAK, END OF 16TH CENTURY

Height : 9' 6" Width : 5' 6"

Victoria and Albert Museum

88

CARPET (UPPER AND LOWER BORDERS NOT REPRODUCED)
Wool pile
ANATOLIAN, USHAK, LATE 16TH—EARLY 17TH CENTURY
Height : 17′ 4″   Width : 8′ 2″

Victoria and Albert Museum

89

CARPET (DETAIL)

Wool pile

ANATOLIAN, USHAK, EARLY 17TH CENTURY

Height (whole carpet) : 7′ 8 1/4″ Width : 4′ 1/4″

Protestant Church of Brassó (Transylvania)

90

CARPET (UPPER BORDER NOT REPRODUCED)

Wool pile

TURKISH, LATE 16TH—EARLY 17TH CENTURY

Height : 12′ 10″   Width : 8′ 7″

Victoria and Albert Museum

91

CARPET

Wool pile

<small>ANATOLIAN, USHAK DISTRICT, 16TH CENTURY</small>

Height : 5′ 11 3/8″   Width : 4′ 8 7/8″

Protestant Church of Szasz-Hermany (Transylvania)

92

PRAYER RUG

Wool pile

ANATOLIAN, 17TH CENTURY

Height : 5′ 9 3/4″   Width : 3′ 11″

Protestant Church of Brassó (Transylvania)

93

PRAYER RUG

ANATOLIAN, BERGAMA, 17TH CENTURY

Height : 5' 6 1/4" Width : 3' 9 3/4"

Brukenthal Museum, Nagyszeben (Transylvania)

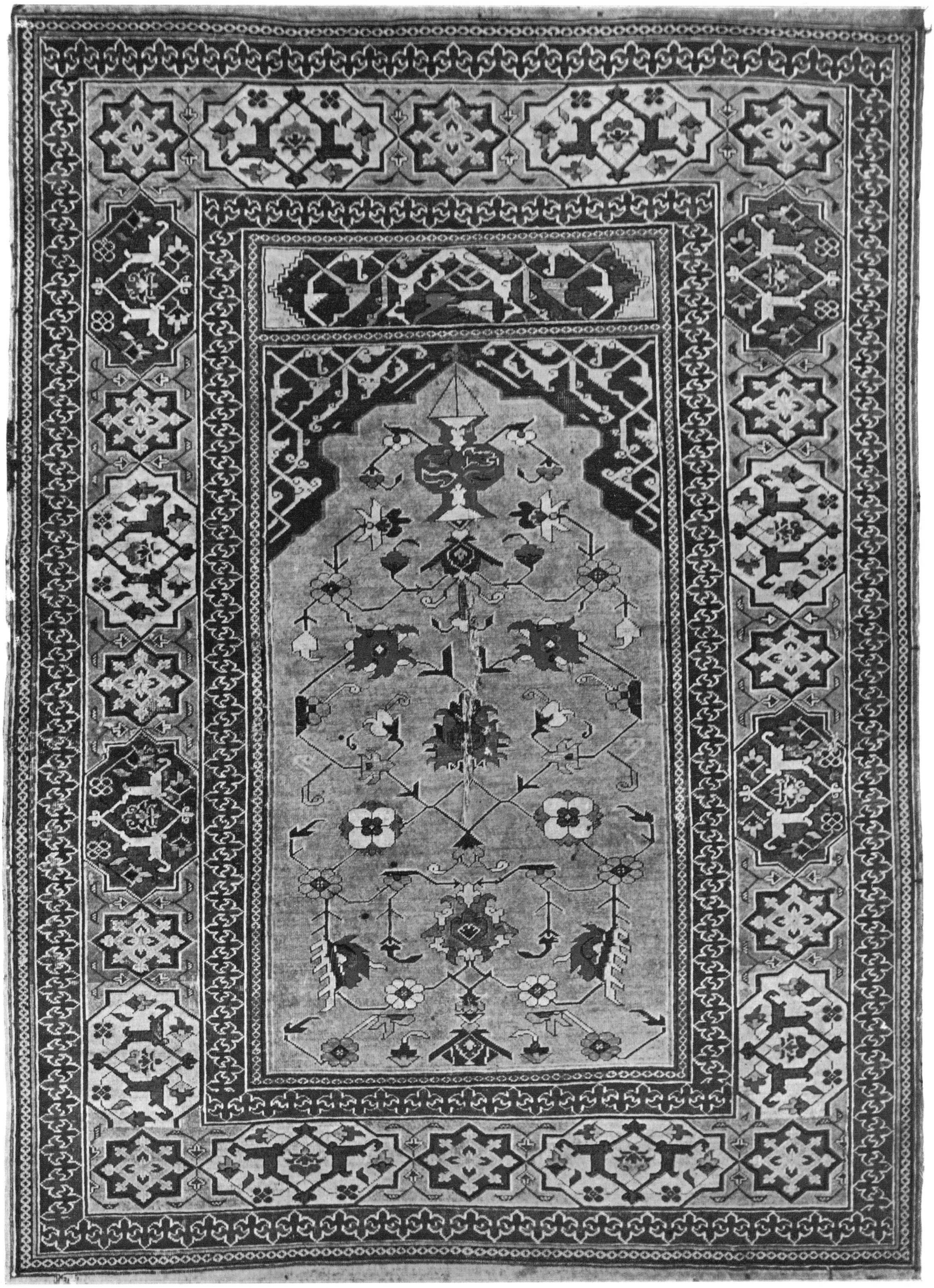

94

CARPET

Wool pile enriched with metal thread

TURKISH 18TH CENTURY

Height : 7′ 7″   Width : 5′ 5″

Victoria and Albert Museum (Salting Bequest)

95

CARPET (FRAGMENT)

Wool pile

INDIAN (MUGHAL), LATE 16TH CENTURY

Height : 3' 11 1/16" Width : 5' 2 3/4"

Musée des Arts Décoratifs

96

CARPET

Wool pile

INDIAN (MUGHAL), 18TH CENTURY

Height : 6′ 4″   Width : 4′ 8″

Victoria and Albert Museum

97

NUSHIRWAN REWARDS THE YOUNG BUZURJMIHR
Miniature from a manuscript of the Shah Nameh of Firdausi
PERSIAN (TABRIZ), ABOUT 1340

Present owner unknown (ex Demotte Collection)

98

THE MEETING OF PRINCE HUMAY AND PRINCESS HUMAYUN
Miniature from a manuscript of the Khamseh of Khwaju Kirmani
PERSIAN (HERAT), ABOUT 1430
Musée des Arts Décoratifs

99

SHEPHERD WITH A GOAT

INDIAN (MUGHAL SCHOOL UNDER PERSIAN INFLUENCE), LATE 17TH CENTURY

Present owner unknown (ex Demotte Collection)